A MAN OF INTEGRITY

A Collection of Letters to Heaven

Lori Myers

Copyright © 2023 Lori Myers

All rights reserved. No part of this book may be reproduced or used in any manner without written permission of the copyright owner except for the use of quotations in a book review.

This book is based on real people and circumstances. The author has taken some creative liberties to tell the stories. Occasionally, dialogue consistent with the character of the person speaking has been supplemented. All persons within are actual individuals; there are no composite characters.

Scripture taken from THE HOLY BIBLE, NEW INTERNATIONAL VERSION®. Copyright©

1973, 1978, 1984, 2011 by Biblica, Inc.™. Used by permission of Zondervan.

First paperback edition 2023

ISBN: 978-1-7364865-8-0 (Paperback)

Cover design and interior formatting by *Hannah Linder Designs*

www.lorimyersbooks.com

To my dad, Jack, who brightened our lives in so many ways. Thank you for your laughter, wisdom, and love.

And to my mom, Marty, and my siblings, Kim, Jeff, Craig, and Jackie, who shared and shaped so many precious childhood memories.

A MAN IS SOMEONE WHO HAS

... broad enough shoulders to carry the burden,
yet soft enough to cradle a loved one
... a touch that can soothe a frightened heart
... a smile that can warm the darkest places
... a quiet contentment and is at peace with himself
... strong enough arms to protect and defend,
yet gentle enough to feel safe and secure in
... the time to listen with genuine interest
... the patience to settle and calm anxiousness
... compassion with no bond to pride
... eyes that can speak without using words,
yet not afraid to shed a tear when his heart is touched
... a sense of humor that can bring a smile to anyone
....direction that satisfies himself and does not harm others
... values that have Jesus in the center
... integrity that guides his decisions
... conviction and truth when he speaks,
yet never misses an opportunity to say something kind
... freely given with no expectation of a return
... love to give without personal gain
... humbled himself and feels no less a man for doing so
... found his place in the world and gives the glory to God.

Lori Myers

CONTENTS

Author's Preamble	vii
Introduction	ix
1. Love	1
2. Kindness	5
3. Gentleness	9
4. Dutifulness	16
5. Generosity	21
6. Resourcefulness	24
7. Humor	28
8. Ethics	32
9. Selflessness	37
10. Wisdom	42
11. Industry	47
12. Justice	51
13. Joyfulness	57
14. Honor	60
15. Vigilance	63
16. Vulnerability (Part I)	66
17. Vulnerability (Part II)	71
18. Integrity	79
19. A Letter from Dad	88
20. The Last Word	90
More on ALS and the Intimate Impact	93
Acknowledgments	97
Other Books by Lori Myers	99
About the Author	101

AUTHOR'S PREAMBLE

My father was—and will always be—special to me. I write this book, a compilation of letters to him, from my perspective, my memories, and my love for him. In doing so, I will choose details, words, and images to help readers understand my perspective, though, can we ever really *know* someone's perspective? Others who knew and loved my daddy have different details, memories, and experiences. That's okay. That's what makes our relationships treasured ones; they are unique to each pair. Thank you, Dad, for your lessons as I remember them and live them out.

INTRODUCTION

I begin at the end. For this, my collection of letters to my favorite person—a man of *integrity*—it's the only logical place to start. It's also where my regret lies.

I gave my dad's eulogy on December 22, 2009, two days after his death. Jack W. Trainham, my dad, had succumbed to amyotrophic lateral sclerosis (ALS), otherwise known as Lou Gehrig's disease, just seven months after his diagnosis.

As the disease progressed, my dad joined a devastating minority—the 5 to 10 percent of those with ALS who lose their ability to speak. Though he couldn't use his words, he continued to pour into his family. My mom, my siblings, and I were the center of his world before the diagnosis and after, and no disease could, or would, ever change that.

Not just a man of integrity, my dad was a man of many virtues, from a time and generation when virtues needed no definitions and were never questioned but merely taught. Perhaps without realizing he was doing so, my dad was teaching his children how to become our best selves. I am the oldest of his and my mom's five children. I don't say this to imply I know more or learned more than my siblings or that this book is "my thing" alone.

I write these letters to my dad out of love. But I also write these letters because of regret. After his death, I realized there was so much more I wanted—needed—to say to him. So much more I wanted to learn . . .

As a gift to us both, I shed these letters like tears, believing that from his position in Heaven, he is looking down and smiling. Knowing, as a man of integrity, he lived as a good and faithful servant to God's call.

As I said, I start with the ending first, my eulogy for him:

Christmas is when we celebrate the birth of our Savior. This is Dad's favorite time of year. How fitting he should join the Father during this time of blessed celebration.

Today, let us celebrate the life of a wonderful husband, father, and grandfather.

What words can capture the depth of the love he had for us? What sacrifice could equal what he would willingly give up for us? What time could we spend that would satisfy OUR need to be with him?

The answers to these questions are testimony to the life he led. No measure too great, no gift too small, no expression too slight. Nothing can compare to his unselfish love for Mom, his children, his grandchildren, and their children.

One may say Dad was quiet and passive, perhaps unassuming. What these descriptions represent are modesty and humility—VIRTUES he lived by—not by his words, but by his actions. Even when faced with the inability to speak, he didn't wish for a louder voice but for neater handwriting. This is but a small example of the humble man he was.

The true character of a man is not measured by how he sees himself, but by how he is seen by others. Those who knew him called him gentle, kind, and caring—[also] a prankster, a storyteller, an all-around loving husband and father.

As I [remember] all the special stories of Jack, Dad, and Bumpa that each of us have—some private, some shared—[I realize] there are so many that it's impossible to find a handful that speak to the essence of him. Another exceptional testimony to his life.

Each of us carries a part of him. Mom, remember how

Dad drew our family tree and said, "Look what we did?" Look around and see His greatest point of pride: the family you both created, the family that will carry us through.

How do you celebrate a life as special as his? You do it by living as [that person] would have wanted you to, with honesty, fairness, compassion, and kindness. This is his legacy, the everlasting testimony of the man he was.

As we are reminded of the fragility of our human [selves], let us be comforted by the fact that our earthly journey is but a blimp in time and that one day, [we] will be rejoined with Dad for eternity.

I believe the poem by Henry Scott Holland speaks perfectly to what Dad wants written on our hearts [I've included a couple of lines]:

I have only slipped away into the next room.
I am I and you are you.
Whatever we were to each other
we still are.

We love you, POP!

The words that day weren't many. For a eulogy, it was on the short side. I didn't want to take up too much time or have others think I was being long-winded or selfish, that my time up there in front of the few who could attend his funeral was a way for me to take over as the oldest child. Because I didn't say everything I wanted to say then, I consider this book my extended eulogy, an addendum, composed of all the words I never gave myself the chance to say. These letters are also the memories I want to keep reliving. And they hold all the love I felt, and still feel, for my dad.

One last thing before we begin, I am a word nerd and a self-professed analytical researcher. So each "chapter" begins with my definition of the virtue that letter highlights, along with brief origin information. Most of that etymology info came from etymonline.com. I hope you find this part of the book as fascinating as I do. If not, feel free to skip to the letter. Regardless of your path through this book, may every word pierce your heart and mind for the better.

Here's to no more regrets, Dad.

1

LOVE

Being deeply loved by someone gives you strength, while loving someone deeply gives you courage. (Lao Tzu)

My Definition: A feeling comprising care, intimacy, attraction, cherishing, enjoyment, comfort, tenderness, and devotion. Though, honestly, there is no combination of words that adequately defines love. You just know it when you have it. Note: Many believe cultural differences in conceptualizing love prevents a universal definition.

Origin: Ancient Greeks identified three forms of love; brotherly love, feelings for one's children and the feelings for one's spouse is *agapē* love.

Dear Dad,

Not a day goes by that you're not with me, just like the poem I read at your funeral says. Deep, emotional revelations still come—some large, some small, some filled with tears, most filled with laughter, and, sometimes still, some filled with guilt. That last one is the one that gets me. I had so much more to say to you, Dad. Through these letters I've written to you, I hope you and I can show people how important love is, how important words are, and how important our loved ones will always be to us.

Many of the virtues I hold dear are those you imparted to me. Not so much in words—that's not how we loved in our home, was it?—but by your actions. Though we weren't the family that embraced or blew kisses, though we weren't the family that shouted "I love you" as we walked out the door, I never thought love wasn't part of our family. And not just a part . . . the primary part. You showed me your love in the ways you knew how, through acts of service and quality time. You were there, Dad. Always. Always doing what needed to be done. You were our chef. Our taxi driver. Our cheerleader. Our coach. And in all those roles, the virtues you held dear poured out. Because of this, what I thought was inherently me, in many ways, is really a mirror image of you.

Dad, I co-published a book earlier this year. It's a collection of poetry and short stories. In it, I wrote you my first letter. We could call it the foreword to this book of letters to you. The letter is titled, "Why Do We Love?" I hope you like it, Dad.

> *Strength doesn't need to be loud, overbearing, in your face;*
> *it can be quiet, steady, and resilient.*
> *Kindness doesn't need recognition or any motivation;*
> *it can show love in the simplest, subtle, yet impactful ways.*
> *Duty isn't old fashioned or out of style;*
> *it grounds us to purposes higher than our own—*
> *faith, family, and community.*
> *Humor doesn't need to be vulgar, cruel, or at someone's expense;*
> *it can be a good practical joke that gives everyone a hearty laugh.*
> *Love doesn't always show up as flowers and chocolates;*
> *it may not come with words,*
> *but it's always there to listen, to guide, to counsel, to uplift.*

I like to believe the here and the hereafter are only separated by an unseen curtain. I hope you can hear me from your heavenly place. I'm pretty sure I never truly thanked you or gave you the credit you deserved for everything you did as a dad, a family man. I am thankful and blessed beyond measure for all the love you gave in so many ways.

Know that your love is your legacy!

Lori

KINDNESS

Kindness is the sincere and voluntary use of one's time, talent, and resources to better the lives of others, one's own life, and the world through genuine acts of love, compassion, generosity, and service. (Unknown)

My Definition: Friendliness with consideration; benevolence.

Origin of Kind: Middle English *kinde*, from Old English *(ge)cynde*, meaning "natural, native, innate," originally, "with the feeling of relatives for each other."

Dad,

I never remember you specifically teaching us to be kind. Not with words anyway. I always knew what kindness was by the way you lived your life. You often communicated this virtue in the simplest ways, like planting all those trees for Mom and never complaining about the work it took to do so. Instead, you marveled at how beautiful they were when they bloomed, always giving Mom the credit.

And remember the time you had a station wagon full of kids on the way home from the public pool—Schiller Park—and you spotted a woman on the side of the road, standing next to her car with the flat tire? She was dressed in a long skirt and her hairdo was the common flip worn by women in the late sixties. My brothers and sisters and I (ranging from five to eight years old) probably still smelled like chlorine, still wore our swimsuits, and likely weren't buckled in since backseat safety belts had yet to be a thing in those station wagons! You didn't hesitate to pull over and help the woman change that tire. Even if we hadn't had our bologna sandwiches already, you would've stopped. Hungry bellies could wait until after serving someone in need. You told us to settle down, jumped out of the car, and jumped into action to change the tire.

Afterward, we asked you if you knew the woman.

"No," you said. "She just needed help." The message was clear. Kindness always wins, no matter who you're offering it to. One of my brothers made a comment about how pretty she was.

"Let's not tell Mom about that part," you said with a chuckle.

I don't know what your official "love language" was, Dad, though I'm sure acts of service had to have been high on the list. It was all the little things you did to take care of us, the acts of kindness—making dinner for our family on most nights (even in those days when men didn't do that), driving everyone anywhere they needed to go (not sure how you juggled that every day), spending countless hours working in the rock garden to make our yard beautiful, playing Parcheesi with giggling teenagers who wouldn't pay attention, apologizing after administering a punishment you felt was too harsh, and sharing your life stories to help make kids (us and our friends) better people. It was changing a tire at a moment's notice for a stranded woman on the side of the road—"pretty" or not.

Sometimes, kindness is mistaken for weakness. Not so for you. It was never a choice but a way of life. And because of that lifestyle, kindness is rooted in me and has been since my earliest memories. I once spent an entire year posting kindness quotes in my professional network to share with others. That was because of you. I'm eternally thankful for how you showed me the genuine value of (and the reward for) being kind.

Thank you, Dad.

Lori

3

GENTLENESS

Gentleness is the ability to bear reproaches and slights with moderation, and not to embark on revenge quickly, and not to be easily provoked to anger, but be free from bitterness and contentiousness, having tranquility and stability in the spirit. (Aristotle)

My Definition: Showing a kind and quiet nature; not harsh or violent.

Origin: From the early thirteenth century, *gentile*, *gentle* meant "well-born, of noble rank or family," and was derived from Old French, *gentil/jentil*, meaning "high-born, worthy, noble, of good family; courageous, valiant; fine, good, fair."

Dear Pop,

We can't talk about kindness without talking about gentleness, can we? I have a special memory to share with you. I think it's one you'll remember too. It was the day I learned there was no Santa. Do you remember, Dad? You handled it so well, with a gentleness only you could provide, and at a time when another adult in my life wasn't so gentle.

It was the week before Christmas and the last day of school before the holiday break. Everyone could feel the dynamic energy in Miss Venner's third-grade class: the chatter, the giggling, the fidgeting in our seats. No one could sit still!

Shortly before class was dismissed, Miss Venner got our attention in her usual way. With a high-pitched shrill, she yelled, "Class! Settle down!" At once, we snapped into place. With a deep breath, she continued, "Who in the class still believes in Santa Claus?"

There was absolute silence. It was the kind of silence that causes its own noise inside your head. *Buzzzz.* Heads turned to and fro to see who had dared to raise their hand. After all, by the third grade, we had learned it was far better to be part of the crowd than to be different or, worse, wrong.

As a Santa-believing juvenile, my hand had inched toward the popcorn ceiling. But when I noticed no one else's hand moving skyward, I tugged it back onto my lap as my face turned red. No one else moved, except for Bobby. I give him credit; his hand had shot up straight and determined.

Miss Venner nodded for Bobby to put his hand down. Then, with authority, she told us, mere eight- and nine-year-olds, that whoever still believed in Santa Claus was a baby. That by the third grade, we should be "grown up enough not to believe in fairy-tales." My heart stuttered with her words. *What?*

From that point forward, I heard nothing else from that unkind teacher or my classmates. My head swam with all the thoughts an eight-year-old has about make-believe, happy endings, and truth. Suddenly, I didn't know up from down or right from left.

My walk home from school that day was a long one. When I turned down Kenwood Avenue, my feet jumped alive, and I ran, determined to find out the truth. I burst into the house, sprinting from room to room, trying to find you and Mom.

As soon as I saw you both, the tears erupted, skidding down my face. There weren't just tears, either, but a sniffly, hiccupping, can't-catch-your-breath kind of crying instead. I'm sure I started blurting out all kinds of things that sounded like gibberish to you and Mom.

"What do you mean there isn't a Santa Claus?"

"Why didn't you tell me the truth?"

"I am not a baby!"

Dad, you walked over to me, put your arms around me, and gently told me to slow down and take a breath. And I did.

Once I calmed down, I could explain what happened in class. Mom wanted to march right up to that school and have words with that teacher. But Dad, you reminded her school was closed for the holiday, and that any conversation would have to wait until after the break.

You took a different approach. Rather than looking to punish Miss Venner for being so insensitive (because she was) and overstepping her bounds (because she did), you focused on my disappointment. You sat down next to me and explained the true meaning of Christmas. You told me that Christmas is about celebrating the birth of our Lord, Jesus. Of course, I knew these things from Sunday school class, but you helped me understand how Santa fit into that story.

I loved how you explained that Santa Claus helped children understand the world of natural consequences, where rewards come for doing the right thing. A world where giving often feels better than receiving. And I'll never forget those lessons.

"Though he isn't real, what he represents is how we can be generous, thoughtful, and kind," you said. Your voice was so gentle, Dad. You told me I was a "big girl" now, and that made me feel special, the opposite of a "baby." My job was to keep Santa alive and help with the grown-up responsibility of making Christmas fun for the little ones, my younger siblings. I was thrilled to hear this grown-up job now included me! And you swore me to secrecy, making me part of the bigger picture with a promise. After all, my brothers and sisters deserved to experience the wonder I had once had.

In those moments next to you on the couch, I knew I was part of something more important than the "Santa Claus story." I had been entrusted to share part of *your* responsibilities, Dad. I probably also felt I had the upper hand over the younger kids!

That year, Mom let me help wrap presents, and I was sworn into another secret; I couldn't tell my siblings what they were getting. Not even a hint. The rest of the week was filled with Christmas shopping, caroling, baking cookies, and stringing popcorn for the tree.

Christmas Eve was always a big deal in our family because it was also Kim's birthday. We'd have a big dinner and a homemade birthday cake for my little sister. Right after dinner, you would start announcing the "Santa sightings," according to the NORAD tracking system.

The excitement built as we watched the clock moving toward midnight that year. When it was close to bedtime, we heard the clear chime of jingle bells. You looked out the window and said, "I believe Santa's right down the street!"

That was our cue.

After our cheers, we made a mad dash for the stairs and hopped into bed. My little brothers chatted away.

"Do you think Santa's that close?"

"What if I can't fall asleep?"

Dad, I'll never forget how you whispered up the stairs, letting us know Santa would come only when we were fast asleep. And so our mouths and eyes closed.

But then you called for me to come downstairs for a minute. There in the living room was a brand new organ, complete with a book of Christmas songs. You told me how proud you and Mom were of me for being such a big girl. Again, your gentleness made everything perfect.

I now know you wanted me to have a special moment, one where you could give that wonderful gift to me! As I sat on the bench thumbing through the music book, I knew the best song that night would be "Silent Night." And you let me play it—several times. Though, I had to do it quietly!

> *Silent night, holy night*
> *All is calm and all is bright*

Dad, I'm so thankful you turned a heartbreaking and embarrassing situation around to make me feel chosen and mature. What my teacher had done could have left a huge hole in my heart. Instead, you focused on me. You showed me how important it is to think of others, to give to others, and to help make special memories. That is how you approached all of life, your full yet quiet nature on display. And you taught me to be my best in any (every!) situation.

Because of you, Dad, Christmas is my favorite holiday.

4

DUTIFULNESS

I came to realize that life lived to help others is the only one that matters, and that it is my duty. This is my highest and best use as a human. (Ben Stein)

My Definition: A respect for the natural order—socially, legally, and religiously—and includes the ideas of patriotism and devotion to others.

Origin: From the late fourteenth century Anglo-French word, *duete*, meaning, "obligatory service, that which ought to be done," or "the force of that which is morally right," which came from Old French *deu, or* "due, owed."

Dear Dad,

A few months after you passed away, I joined a reminiscence writing course. I had signed up before you left us, not knowing you would be gone when the classes began. The assignments were tough as my emotions were raw; the sting was deep, and our daily visits had ended.

The writing instructor guided us through the process using her experiences and memories. This made the lessons poignant, almost tangible. My heart ached with grief, and I wasn't sure if I could do it. I'd heard that when you experience the loss of someone dear, you joined a unique club, but I never really got it . . . until then.

The assignments required much reflection and emotional endurance. Amazingly, as my pen flowed, I found great comfort in revisiting the happier times in my life. To "compare and contrast" became therapeutic as I wrestled with your death but focused on our life together. Dad, it brought me such joy to relive those happy memories that meant so much to me, to us. Memories that helped inform who I am today, and you were such a big part of that.

I was rummaging through old family photos to help me through the course when I found a commendation you received when you were a mere twenty years old. Commander Colonel John H.

Kunkel Jr. of the United States Air Force had nominated you as the "Outstanding Airman" of the 3906th Air Police Squadron for the period between March 1, 1957 and August 31, 1957.

When I read the letter, a sense of pride puffed up my grieving heart. Barely out of your teens, you were displaying the characteristics of a seasoned man. The commander used words like loyalty, accomplishment, sound judgment, devotion, high moral standards, initiative, resourcefulness, and tact.

I knew what these words meant. They painted a picture of your character. *You valued duty—duty to God, country, family, and your value-system.*

Duty is not a fun word, but it's a powerful one. It speaks to your maturity and the respect you offered your chain of command, especially at such a young age. You've always had a way with people, a courtesy that came through no matter who they were, what they had done, or what you may have thought about them. You acted without offending, in accordance with what your chain of command ordered and what your responsibilities were.

When you left the military, it may have been why it was so easy to value duty to God. And why so many people loved you. You touched lives with your gentle yet authoritative language, your wise advice, and a dedication to your responsibilities, even during correction, even in controversial issues. You not only mastered obedience, you mastered tact.

And I felt the privilege of being on the receiving end of what you learned throughout your life about this virtue. It's no surprise to me, Dad, that Mom fell for you not long after you received this recognition.

Headquarters
3906th Air Base Group
APO-117 USAF

HPS

October 23, 1957

SUBJECT: Outstanding Airman Achievement Award

TO: Airman Second Class Jack W. Trainham AF-11287076
3906th Air Police Squadron
APO 117, USAF

1. I take great pleasure in informing you that you have been selected as the "Outstanding Airman" of the 3906th Air Police Squadron for the period March 1, 1957 to August 31, 1957.

2. Your selection as the "Outstanding Airman" of the Squadron was made by a board of Officers and Non-Commissioned Officers of your Organization. The decision to nominate you for this award was based upon your outstanding personal appearance, the high degree of initiative displayed by you in the accomplishment of assigned duties, the tact and sound judgement you have used in your association with military and civilian personnel, loyalty to your Unit, and your high standard of off-duty conduct.

3. Your devotion to duty and rigid adherence to the highest code of ethics and moral standards reflect great credit upon you and the United States Air Force. Your willingness, resourcefulness, and initiative have indicated you are most deserving of this honor.

4. I congratulate you on the fine example you have set for all Airmen in the 3906th Air Police Squadron.

JOHN H. KUNKEL JR.
Colonel, USAF
Commander

5

GENEROSITY

We would be wise to accumulate things for the sole purpose of sharing their joy with others. (Barbara Lynn-Vannoy)

My Definition: Abundantly giving of time, talent, and treasures.

Origin: From the Latin word *generosus*, meaning "of noble birth". Its contemporary meaning is, "open-handedness and giving to others."

Dad,

Do you remember our pseudo fireplace at Christmastime? I'll never forget when you started this funny little tradition. Our home had no official fireplace, and for a family with young children at Christmas, that just wouldn't do. Where would Santa come from? Where would the stockings hang?

So you bought orange, yellow, and red crepe paper to replicate a fire, then you bought some black paper for the fireplace frame and created a cozy mirage in our living room. Complete with a faux mantle, the crepe paper appeared to be flames dancing inside a fireplace.

But, Dad, you didn't stop there! You pinned our stockings to the wall, making them appear to hang from the "mantle!"

After Christmas every year, you repaired the wall where the pinholes were, only to do it all over again the following year.

Another generous tradition that we've continued with our families, Dad, comes complete with the poignant smells that trigger so many memories of our childhood. You and Mom would fill our stockings with tangerines and ribbon candy. We'd also have access to a bowl of walnuts that we learned how to open with a nutcracker. I can't let a Christmas go by without sniffing a tangerine or enjoying ribbon candy. Oh, the citrusy and sugary sweetness! By the way, Dad, the only place to buy ribbon candy now is on Amazon. It's expensive, but we do it nonetheless. Those smells remind me you're still with us.

But perhaps the most generous memory I recall is that you usually had only one present under the tree with your name on it. Those times growing up when we didn't have much, you wouldn't let your kids go without. I remember there were some Christmases where you didn't have a single gift at all. But your kids always did.

Maybe there are many dads who would give up this much for their children. But as kids, we didn't know this. *We didn't notice what you had sacrificed.* We only saw our toys—our surplus—because there were plenty of gifts under the tree with our names on them. It wasn't until we got much older that we noticed you weren't opening presents too. That's how incredible you made our Christmases . . . our entire lives.

Later, after your death, I asked Mom why Christmas was always so important to you. She said it was because you never had a Christmas growing up.

Dad, you were amazing! You still are. Your traditions and generosity live on in each of your children and grandchildren.

6

RESOURCEFULNESS

It's not about the resources you have available. It's about the resourcefulness you have within you. (Tony Robbins)

My Definition: The ability to find clever ways to overcome difficulties or obstacles.

Origin: From the Old French word *resourdre*, meaning "to rally, raise again," which came from the Latin word *resurgere*, "rise again."

Pop,

Do you mind if I tell this story? I don't think you will. It ended up being one of the greatest lessons you taught us, perhaps without even realizing it. You were just living the only way you knew how to live, but many years later, I'd look back and wonder how you made such a scary, difficult situation seem safe and fun.

When I was ten, the employees at the factory where you worked went on a labor strike. In those days, there were no unemployment benefits when unions went on strike. It seemed like just a few weeks later that Mom was let go from her job at General Electric. Since the company eliminated the plant's television division, she received unemployment.

I don't know the amount of those weekly checks, Dad, but somehow, between her unemployment checks and the money you brought in from the odd jobs you found, there was enough for food and rent.

Before all this happened, you and Mom had purchased furniture and appliances on credit. Obviously, after prioritizing our greatest needs, paying those credit card bills came after food and rent. There just was not enough money to stretch that far, so we eventually lost those things—first being the living room furniture.

But the kids never heard you express any despair. Instead, you made a game of it. As the furniture was removed from our home, you grabbed the biggest blanket we had and stretched it out on the living room floor. You told us watching TV while seated on the floor was like going to the drive-in movies. Sometimes, we'd leave the TV off and have a picnic while playing a game.

Then we lost our refrigerator, but you remained resourceful. With the long winters in Syracuse, New York, you built up a small snowbank on the back porch so we had a place for our milk and eggs.

Next, we lost our car. I'm sure this was devastating to you and Mom. But to us kids, it did not seem like a big deal. When we needed groceries, you simply grabbed the wooden sled and walked to the grocery store, always taking one or two of us to help. I don't know if you knew this—I'm sure I didn't tell you with words—but I loved those walks in the snow, especially when it was dark. When the air was crisp, and I heard the crunch of the snow under my boots, everything seemed right in the world. Even though we had no furniture, no appliances, and no car, the world felt so quiet—and me, I felt so at peace!

That was because of you, Dad.

I never remember a time when I was afraid. Sure, I knew our circumstances were not great, but I always felt safe, cared for, and loved. I am certain the resiliency and resourcefulness I tap into when facing hardships now were forged in those early days. I am sure you had the weight of the world on you—a wife and five kids on a meager income. Yet you never showed us the fear you must have felt. Instead, you exhibited courage!

I know you grew up with many hardships, Dad. Your mother's love and commitment to family set the example that made you the man you were. And your love and commitment to us, the example you set for us, made me the person I am today.

This was not our life for long. Thankfully, it was only for a season. But it was your resiliency and resourcefulness that got us through that season. The love you imprinted on me carries on today, in me and in my children—your grandchildren. Thank you, Dad, for being strong, thoughtful, and caring. For rallying us in times of need. And for loving us like you did!

7

HUMOR

While spending a lifetime finding the answer, along the way I discovered humor makes the journey a lot more enjoyable.
(Patricia Heller)

My Definition: A summation of comics, jokes, pranks, silliness, and amusement; wittiness.

Origin: From the modern French, the sense of "amusing quality, funniness, jocular turn of mind" is first recorded in the 1680s, probably from the meaning, "whim, caprice" as determined by state of mind (Old French 1560s).

Dear Dad,

The warm summers and still-warm fall days were some of the most special for me growing up. We kids would enjoy outdoor childhood games with our friends and neighbors—games like dodgeball, kickball, and my favorite, hide-and-seek. I want to share with you something I wrote recently, long after you left this earth, about a memory I have from the summer I turned thirteen. It comes from another book I wrote called *Glimpses of Tenderness*, and inside Chapter 1, Sounds of Home, it says this:

> *Twilight is approaching. Twelve neighborhood kids hurry through dinner. Everyone is anxious to start the nightly game of hide-and-seek. My house is the perfect place to play. It sits in the middle of a city park, surrounded by large trees and dense bushes. The absence of streetlights adds to the neighborhood's darkness. Oh, how we love the thrill of playing a game where you hide in the dark!*
>
> *The best hiding spots are well known. Each child hoping to find that one place where he can fake out the "seeker." Darkness comes. We gather in the field restlessly waiting to start the game.*
>
> *Throughout the game, I am laser-focused on avoiding that tap on the shoulder, accompanied by a loud shout of "You're it!"*

[Back then, Dad was part of our game.] *He peeks out of the living room window. Always the prankster, he enjoys times when he can surprise us. More times than not, his goal is to scare us.* [Trust me, he was good at that.] *He carefully creeps out of the house through the cellar door. He slides behind an eight-foot rock wall that towers on the opposite side of the field where we play. No one hides behind that old wall because it is in plain sight.*

As another game starts, frenzied kids, all trying to avoid being caught, run in every direction. Dad uses this chaotic moment to move into position. He plans to jump out at just the right moment to scare as many kids as possible. And boy, does he!

Imagine a stampede of kids taking off at break speed, all trying to get to the safety of the nearest house—my house. Though I am first through the door, I quickly find myself underfoot, literally. Every kid in the neighborhood is running over the top of me as I remain sprawled out on the hallway floor. Everyone is screaming for Dad to come help: "Dad!"

"Mr. Trainham!"

"Jack!"

All shouting in unison, including Mom, who heard all the commotion from her spot in the kitchen. [Oh, how we wailed in surprise and disbelief when we found out that Dad was the bogeyman himself! He was always there to save us from whatever stirred in the dark.]

Dad, do you remember that? I miss those days. Do you?

Lori

8

ETHICS

Ethics is a code of values which guide our choices and actions and determine the purpose and course of our lives.
(Ayn Rand)

My Definition: Moral principles, such as fairness, respect, and equity, that govern someone's choices and actions.

Origin: From the 1600s, the plural of the Middle English word *ethik*, meaning "the study of morals."

Hi, Dad,

You were a man of principle—kind and fair—and expected us, as your children, to live by the same standards you set and lived out your entire life. Every day of your life, your values, your ethics, poured out of you like honey from a jar. We all knew you held integrity, accountability, and honesty in the highest regard.

Dad, do you remember how I failed at all three of those values in a single event? I sure do . . .

It was the summer I turned seventeen. A driver's license burned a hole in my wallet, and I could finally drive the family car without a supervising adult. Thrilled with my newfound freedom, I frequently offered to go to the store or pick up my younger brothers and sisters just so I could "take a drive." I felt so grown-up and *in charge* when I was behind the wheel, especially with the window down, the Eagles's "Hotel California" blasting from the speakers, and me . . . singing away.

The errand I offered to run on *that* day was to pick up Mom from work. I arrived a little early, so I parked your car in the hospital's parking garage, near her office. I did some window shopping, then went to see if Mom was ready. She told me to get the car, that she'd be ready by the time I got back. The parking spaces were narrow and painted at an angle. Pulling into the space was easy, but backing out was when trouble found me. Or maybe I found it.

I turned too sharply and backed into a concrete

pillar. As the bumper ground against concrete, I saw your expression in my mind and heard the sound of your disappointment ring in my ears. "I told you to be careful. We only have one car." Those were the words I expected. *What in the world am I going to do?* I thought, assuming the punishment would be severe. That I'd *never* be able to drive again!

On the ride home, I tried to find the courage to tell Mom what had happened, but I chickened out. The longer we drove, the more nervous I grew. Sweat beaded in my armpits and on my forehead. Still, I said nothing.

When we got home, you jumped in the car with us because we needed food from the grocery store. You didn't see the dent and, by then, any courage that had been cowering in my heart had completely disappeared. I didn't say a word.

You dropped Mom and me off at the food store while you ran to do another errand . . . to get the car washed. I didn't know that was where you were going.

When you caught up with us at the grocery store, you chatted with Mom for a few minutes, then asked me how my drive had been earlier. My nerves got the better of me. All I wanted to do was shout out the truth, but I just couldn't find the words. My stomach tied itself into knots.

Then you said you'd just washed the car and found a dent in the bumper.

My heart beat wildly in my chest. You asked me if I knew what had happened to the car. That was my chance to come clean, but I lied, pretending I knew nothing about the dent.

I should not have been surprised by how well you knew my mannerisms, Dad. You were, after all, my daddy. I couldn't look you in the eye; I was fidgety and talked like a magpie, and you instantly picked up on my deceit. In your typical way, you calmly asked me to get some ice cream while you and Mom went to the checkout line. I think you knew that would be the longest walk of my life.

When I came back to the front of the store, you said, "Think again about your answer, Lori." I knew I had to do the right thing at that point, no matter what punishment awaited. Anything would be better than losing more of your trust. I confessed, but I tried to position myself in a better light, as blamelessly as possible. Well, we both know that didn't help the situation. Now I was shirking my responsibility for the accident. You stopped me before I could dig my hole any deeper.

I lost my driving privileges for the rest of the summer—not because I had an accident. I learned later that I would have been forgiven. I lost my driving privilege because I had been dishonest and did not own up to my mistake. Not being able to drive was not nearly as painful as having lost some of your trust, Dad. I'm sure you knew that.

Incredibly, through my lies, you remained kind and fair, using a humble approach while handling the situation. This was a teaching moment. There was no shouting, no overreacting, and no guilt trip. You gave me a way to redeem myself and maintain some dignity—a quiet pause during a long walk to get ice cream was just enough time to think about my actions and to forever embed in my character the importance of the ethics you had instilled in me.

Mom reminded me recently that one of your favorite things to say to us when we did something wrong was, "Now, was that the right thing to do?" Dad, I see now that's a question you used to get us to think. You never engaged with us in a scolding lecture.

Thank you, Dad. Thank you for your values and your fair and compassionate parenting. You were the best teacher I ever had.

Lori

9

SELFLESSNESS

It is under the greatest adversity that there exists the greatest potential for doing good, both for oneself and others.
(Dalai Lama XIV)

My Definition: A concern with the needs and wishes of others more than with one's own.

Origin: In 1821, coined from the Old English word for *self*, *sylf* (West Saxon) or *seolf* (Anglian), meaning, "one's own person, -self; own, personal; same, identical." Then made a noun.

It's me again, Dad,
    I need to set the scene for those who are taking a

peek at these letters I've written to you. So this first part is for them, okay?

One of our favorite family traditions was going to the drive-in movies in the summer. Perhaps it was a place that brought back fond memories for my parents of their being teenagers in the fifties. I'm certain my dad enjoyed it just as much, if not more, than we kids did.

Syracuse had four drive-in theaters, one in every direction. Given the choice, the kids picked the one on the north side, which had a playground under the bottom of the enormous screen. Of course, the choice of drive-in was ultimately determined by what was playing on that big screen.

Mom went with us when we were little, but when I was old enough to help with the younger kids, Dad would take us by himself. Sure, I missed Mom, but those were the times when I got the best seat in the house: the front passenger seat. I'd graduated from the blanket on the hard ground that Dad had lain on the driver's side of the car, to keep watch over the kids during the movie.

During one particular movie night—when I was fourteen—as was our routine, we headed out to the north-end drive-in. Dad spread out the blanket and put out a few pillows and a couple of extra blankets for the younger kids. Each of us had our favorite candy in hand, from Sno-Caps and Jujubes to Dad's favorite, Good & Plenty. We made our one trip to the concession stand for a few buckets of popcorn and soft drinks. The younger ones were dressed in their PJs, mostly because it wouldn't be long before they fell asleep, well before the movie was over. This made it easier to carry them straight to bed. I was a teenager, so there would be no PJs in public for me. I could stay awake for the entire movie.

After everything was set up, we all went to the playground to have some fun until the opening commercials started. Of course, we didn't just walk to the playground; it was an all-out race between Dad and five giggling, screaming kids.

"On your mark, get set, GO!" In one shot, we darted from the starting line.

Dad, you always let us take the lead. As we pushed farther and faster, I looked over my shoulder to see where you were. I felt you coming up behind us before I saw you. Then suddenly, you fell to the ground. I reacted, digging my toes into the earth below to stop as quickly as possible, and ran back to help.

You said you'd hit a dip in the ground, something like a pothole. As you got up, I could tell something wasn't right. You made a slight groan, then pursed your lips as if to hold back any other expression. I noticed you cradling your right forearm and walking slowly, as if making sure you wouldn't hit another hole.

"Are you OK, Dad?"

"I'll be fine."

I ushered the kids back to the blanket and settled down just as an animated box of popcorn and a soda bottle danced across the big screen, signaling the start of the film. I ran around the car and jumped into the front seat. Cutting my eyes to the left, I kept watch over you, Dad, to see how you were doing. I'm sure you noticed.

Shortly after the movie started, when I looked over, I saw a tear rolling down your face. I didn't know what was wrong. I asked again if you were OK. Again, you said you'd be fine, but you added, "My arm is hurting, but I don't know what's wrong."

"Taking care of your arm is more important than the movie, Dad. We should go to the hospital to get your arm looked at." My heart raced under my rib cage.

After a few rounds of pleading with you, I went outside and told the kids that you had hurt your arm when we had been racing and that we needed to get you to the hospital to see what was wrong. There wasn't a peep in the bunch. Everyone grabbed up their pillows, blankets, and snacks, then scrambled into the backseats of the station wagon.

When we got to the hospital, a nurse brought you a wheelchair. When you reached for the armrest, we heard a loud *pop*. Your shoulder was dislocated. You're probably shaking your head right now, Dad, up in Heaven, chuckling at the memory of pain since you can't feel it any longer.

Miraculously, when your fingers grabbed ahold of the wheelchair, your shoulder popped back into place. I watched the look of pain on your face vanish. You smiled—*smiled!*—and said you felt much better.

The significance of this story, Dad, is not the fond memory of summer trips to the drive-in movies or the fun-filled routines we had, or even the details of your injury. The point is your selflessness. You had been willing to sit and endure the pain through the duration of the movie so your kids could enjoy a night at the drive-in. That kind of selfless love was not lost on any of us, Dad. This was just one of many situations where I know you sacrificed something for us, often putting our joy ahead of your needs.

Thank you, Dad.

Lori

10

WISDOM

Yesterday I was clever, so I wanted to change the world. Today I am wise, so I am changing myself. (Rumi)

My Definition: Pairing experience and knowledge to use good judgment.

Origin: Compounded from the Old English word *wis, meaning* "earned, sagacious, cunning; sane; prudent, discreet; experienced" and the Old English word *dom,* meaning "statute, judgment."

Dad,

You were the consummate storyteller. Some of your stories were whimsical and fantastical, like the ones about the Easter Bunny, Santa Claus, Bigfoot, and the Tooth Fairy, but most of your stories were what I call "life stories," which you used to help reinforce a lesson. I think of them as Andy Griffith moments. I can still hear Grandma T. and her stories, too, echoing in my memories. I guess that's where you learned the art of storytelling. It runs in the family!

Much of what or how you taught us was connected to events and lessons from your childhood, including teaching us how to swim. Yes, that came with a story too.

Dad, I'd like to share one of your childhood events. It's a sad one. I hope you don't mind.

The day before my dad's ninth birthday, his older brother, Kenny, drowned, along with his friend, C. G., while swimming in the power flume of the Carthage Machine Company. It was believed the boys had decided to take a swim after school. Two of their friends sounded the alarm when they discovered Kenny and C.G.'s clothes near the flume but couldn't find them. It was impossible to drag the flume because of its design, so the company drained the water to about four feet.

My dad's older brother, Thomas, was summoned to the site. He had recently returned home from military service following World War II. Because the water was so murky

> *and no one could see but an inch down, Thomas dove in. He found the boys locked together, likely a case of one boy trying to save the other. The fathers of both boys were at the scene as they watched Thomas and a local police officer administer CPR to no avail.*

I can only imagine the impact this left on you, Dad. Like so many other hard times in your life, you used your hardships as lessons for your own kids.

Every summer, we'd head to the local pool in Schiller Park. The city pool had two diving boards in the twelve-foot-deep end of the pool, one low dive and one high dive. By the time I was eight, I'd mastered both and had become an accomplished swimmer who could dive off both without a spotter.

When Jeff was five, it was his turn to learn how to dive off the low dive. Dad, as with us all, you laid out the order for Jeff's first time off the board by himself. You would go first, and when you were out far enough from the board that he wouldn't land on you, Jeff would go off the board. Then, I'd follow once Jeff was far enough out.

After those instructions, Dad, you dove in. I was behind Jeff in line and could sense my brother's nervousness. He slowly climbed up the stairs, then hesitated. He looked back at me and found my eyes. I told him he would be fine, that you were right there waiting for him. With that empowerment, Jeff ran to the end of the diving board, jumped in, and steadily swam his way toward you.

When I could see he was safely out of the way, I jumped in. When I came up, I could see Jeff paddling faster and more frantically. I heard you shouting to him that it was OK and to continue swimming toward you. When Jeff got close enough to you, in a panic, he grabbed you around the neck with all his might.

As I swam closer, I saw you struggling. Jeff was holding on so tightly, he was causing the both of you to go under. I sprint-swam to get to you. You had taught me to stay behind the frantic swimmer and not let them grab me in the water because you had learned in your childhood that this very thing would happen. So I grabbed ahold of Jeff from behind and pushed him to the side of the pool, then I grabbed you under an arm and pulled you along to the side too.

I don't know that my legs ever pumped water as quickly as they did that day. My only focus was saving my little brother and you. I don't remember being afraid or panicking, just feeling determined. You had taught me and my siblings to swim at an early age because you never wanted us to be afraid of the water, and you taught us what to do to save someone from drowning without sacrificing our own lives.

Dad, you told the story of me rescuing Jeff and you in that pool over and over, always saying how proud you were of me for being brave enough to save you both. As a kid, I was thrilled to be the hero of this story.

As an adult, I'm thankful that you looked at life the way you did, that hardships should become lessons, ones that may someday compel us to show courage when facing our own hardships . . . helping us prevail. You always shared your priceless wisdom!

INDUSTRY

Always do your best. What you plant now,
you will harvest later.
(Og Mandino)

My Definition: Hard work, tenacity, innovative pursuit, clever skill.

Origin: From fourteenth-century Old French *industrie*, meaning "activity; aptitude, experience," or directly from the Latin word *industria*, meaning "diligence, activity, zeal."

My Dear Dad,
My early years were chock-full of countless

simple memories with you. What is amazing about those memories is that during my early childhood, until I was ten, you had four kids in tow. And no matter what we were doing (or getting into), you always seemed happy. I am sure we were a handful, but you never seemed frazzled or short-tempered.

With no planning—that I was aware of—no matter the season, off we would go into new adventures.

In the summer, you would pack us all in the car to get ice cream, then we'd move on to watch planes take off and land near our local airport. Sometimes, it was a trip to the local swimming pool. You even packed us lunch, usually consisting of bologna sandwiches, chips, apples, and Mountain Dew. Remember, Daddy? And if we were good, we would get a freezy pop at the concession stand.

In the fall, you took us to Sainte Marie among the Iroquois (or the French Fort, as locals call it). The fort was a replica of the seventeenth-century Jesuit mission, in the middle of the Onondaga Nation. Though this mission only operated from 1656 to 1658, it served as a living history museum of the mission work from its time. Dad, you were always such a huge history buff. I have no doubt that is where some of us got our passion for history.

Even though you worked hard, we would also

make our annual trip to the pumpkin farm in Homer, New York. You loved to take that drive because the fall foliage painted such an incredible picture along the highways. We'd each get a pumpkin; you'd stock up on fresh apple cider, and we'd buy a bushel of apples, along with all the fixings to make candy apples.

Winter would not be complete without our snow angels and the sturdy snow forts we created after big snowfalls. You would spend hours digging out the perfect location for our forts, and you even included a setting bench made of hard-packed snow. You were always so industrious.

Sometimes, Dad, you would take us to the laundromat. Mom could not hang the laundry outside in the winter, so it was easier to spend Saturdays at the laundromat, catching up on the mountains of dirty clothes a family of six generated. We played on the linoleum floor while you washed and dried load after load. And we never saw you complain.

The Burnet Park Zoo was our first destination after the snow thawed. Once we knew it was warm enough for the animals to be out, we'd beg you to go there to see the monkeys, birds, lions, and tigers. And we'd grab bags of peanuts for the elephants.

I remember the drives we all took, ones filled with stories about our family and silly songs we made up. You gave each of us a color and a city to help us, and we'd do our best to rhyme the words. Remember?

> Lori – Red – Los Angeles
> Kim – Green – Little Old Lady from Pasadena
> Jeff – Blue – Cincinnati
> Craig – Yellow – Philadelphia

I don't know if you aligned them to our personalities, but all we knew or cared about was that it was super fun. You made us feel so special, Dad.

What I learned from all these memories, born through these simple activities, was that anyone can have fun, no matter how little money they have. You taught us how to make people feel special, and you built our confidence and courage by being present, caring, loving, and kind. Even after working so hard during the week.

What you planted in us then, Dad, has reaped a harvest of values we especially learned from you.

Lori

12

JUSTICE

I have always found that mercy bears richer fruits than strict justice. (Abraham Lincoln)

My Definition: The pursuit of fairness, respect, and peace while administering the law or persecuting wrongdoings.

Origin: From mid-twelfth-century Old French word *justice,* meaning "the exercise of authority in vindication of right by assigning reward or punishment," coming directly from the Latin word *iustus,* from the eleventh century, meaning "righteousness, equity."

Dear Dad/Santa,

Christmas was such a special time in our family. That's why so many of my memories seem to have come during the Christmas season. What better time to teach young kids about life lessons, right? I think I hear you chuckling in Heaven.

After I was brought into the "adult realm" of keeping the belief in Santa alive for my younger brothers and sisters, you and Mom swore me to secrecy about where all the presents really came from—you! While that was a lot to put on a kid, I felt ready. After all, I was the first-born and wanted to live up to that title.

And like any good oldest child, I had learned all the benefits that come with that position. For instance, I was skilled in the art of negotiation. I'd use my power of persuasion when I wanted one of the other kids to do my chores, give me one of their toys, or keep a secret from you and Mom. But you already know this about me.

The first Christmas after I was brought into the "real Santa confidence," these two powers—negotiation and persuasion—came into conflict when you and Mom let me in on that year's secret hiding place for all the gifts. As you know, Dad, we lived in a flat, so there weren't many places to hide a bunch of gifts, anyway. But when you told me the unused closet in the back bedroom was the appointed place, I beamed. I knew no one went into that room except you and Mom, since it was Jackie's bedroom. The baby's room. By the way, I love that she was named after you.

I am not sure what came over me, but one day, curiosity bested me, and I went into that closet. I looked at the pile of gifts and marveled at how it almost reached the top of the closet. With wide-open eyes, I memorized as many of the gifts as I could. I wasn't overtly thinking about it as leverage, Dad. I just knew it was powerful information, and that power made me feel so mature.

As I scanned the pile, I took note of who would likely get which gift, including the baby's toys. Then I spied it. There, in plain sight, was the gift I'd been asking for since May 18, my birthday. The Easy Curl hair-setting kit. Even today, I remember the rhyming song from the commercial talking about being a grown-up girl. Oh, Dad, I felt so grown-up right then. I wanted those hot rollers more than any of the other presents put together. You know, I'm not even sure why . . . I was such a gritty girl, enjoying running around outdoors and getting dirty—and I hardly ever combed my hair!

Sure enough, an opportunity came along to barter with Jeff and Craig. They had caught me going into the pantry for cookies before dinner and threatened to tell you. In a panic, I said, "I'll tell you a secret if you don't tell Mom and Dad." They both agreed, and I divulged one of their presents to each of them. I didn't tell them that Santa Claus wasn't a real person or where the presents were hidden. Though, Dad, even now, I hear the justification in my words. I just shared with them one present I knew they were going to get. Then I held my breath for two days, but they kept their word.

Christmas morning finally came. It was the usual flurry of unbridled excitement, a frenzy of presents flying to and fro, along with all the shiny wrapping paper. Finally, we came to the last of the gifts. Something was missing. I searched through the piles of gift wrap and surveyed each sibling's pile of booty. It wasn't there! The Easy Curl hair-setting kit!

You asked all of us if we had a good Christmas, and a resounding "YESSSSS!" erupted from the bunch. My voice was quieter, more like a whisper. Then you looked right at me, Dad, and asked if I'd gotten everything I'd asked Santa for. I looked around as the silence seemed to linger for a time. Then I said, "Yes, yes I did!"

You chuckled and said, "You must've been a very good girl."

All day long, I thought about that Easy Curl gift

and pouted because I didn't get the only thing I really wanted. I tried playing with a new doll then engaged in a game with my sister, but it all fell flat. As flat as my stringy, uncombed hair. At dinner, you asked me why I looked so sad, why I'd been pouting all day. I pondered my response because I didn't want to seem ungrateful. You knew I was holding back and asked me again. Finally, I told you there was something I had asked Santa for but didn't get: the Easy Curl hair-setting kit.

"I thought Santa knew how much I wanted that. I don't know why I didn't get it." Even in my disappointment, I tried to keep up the charade. Then, Dad, you leaned toward me and quietly said, "That's what you get for snooping and for telling your brothers about one of their gifts."

I lost my next breath as my stomach dropped, as if I'd fallen onto my backside. *It must have been my brothers!* I blurted out, "How did you know?"

You told me you had set a booby trap because our flat was so small. That when you found the trap had been snapped, you thought maybe I'd had a moment of weakness. But what really happened was Craig—like he always did—told you I traded a secret for him not telling you about the cookie.

To teach me a lesson, you and Mom held out the gift I wanted most. I slinked away from the table and went into my bedroom. There, on my bed, was the Easy Curl hair-setting kit. You came into the doorway and stood. "I think you've learned your lesson and since you didn't lie about what you did or make excuses, I think you've been punished enough."

Dad, I want you to know . . . I've never snooped since and can keep gift secrets like the best of them!

Lori

JOYFULNESS

If you want to really know higher dimensions of life, there needs to be a constant sense of peacefulness and joyfulness within you.
(Jaggi Vasudev)

My Definition: Living with delight, pleasure, and happiness, no matter the circumstances.

Origin: From the eleventh-century Latin word *gaudia*, plural of *gaudium*, meaning, "joy, gladness, delight."

Written in 2007 for Dad's 70th Birthday

Dear Dad,

Though we're now separated by the curtain that hangs between here and the next life, you are always close in my heart. I hope you know how special you are and always have been to me. As you know, this is the letter I wrote for your seventieth birthday party, included with the family coat of arms we gave you. I hope you experience a double portion of joy as you read it again!

For me, the true measure of a man is the standards one sets. Family first, no matter what. Words have never been necessary; your actions say it all. It just goes to show there aren't many left like you. After all, I had to move all the way to North Carolina and wait until I was forty years old to find one close to you. I make fun and call my Clint "Dad," but in my heart (and everyone else's), I know it's really an honor.

So many of the most wonderful times in my life are memories I have from my childhood and all the special things you did with us. Throughout my whole life, you have made great memories—be it tricks and pranks, going strawberry, apple, and pumpkin picking, or just sitting on the porch as you told us your war stories. My children all feel the same way; you're the greatest "bumpa" around. I hope I can be the grandparent that you are to them.

Here we are, on the brink of Julien's arrival. It's been a while since you've had a little baby around. I sit and daydream about you, me, and him hanging out on the screen porch. I can't wait until he's old enough for you to teach him about the trees and the other things in the garden.

I'm sure you know how much I love you, but to be quite certain, I'll say it just like that: I LOVE YOU, DAD! You are the BEST DAD anyone could wish for or ever have. I am very privileged to call you DAD! HAPPY BIRTHDAY, DAD!!!

Dad, I'll cherish this letter that remains now that you're gone. Julien was just a baby when you passed. But I know you're looking down, relishing in eternal joy, and I want you to know that joy lives here, too, as we think about you.

Lori

14

HONOR

No person was ever honored for what he received. Honor has been the reward for what he gave. (Calvin Coolidge)

My Definition: Abundant respect and great esteem; adherence to what is right or noble; a reputable status.

Origin: From 1200, *onur*, meaning "glory, renown, fame earned," then from the Anglo-French word *honour* and Old French *onor* (*honor*), meaning "honor, dignity, distinction, position; victory, triumph."

Dear Dad,

This letter is a bit difficult to write. As one blogger put it, "Defining honor is like catching the wind—it is all around you, but you can't get your hands on it." Honor is one of those abstract virtues that encompasses an emotional component. *Reverence.*

Honor comes from being honorable, which you were—no doubt. It was part of your identity.

In both life and death, Dad, you earned an honorable position. Not only in my eyes, but in the eyes of everyone you knew and touched. For me, you were the poster child for this virtue: doing what was right, garnering respect in your quiet way, and stepping into some invisible status, which you held with humility. I doubt for one minute any of those things were in the forefront of your mind. Your honor shone through your other virtues, which you held in high regard. (I don't think you ever had even a speeding ticket, Dad!)

That's the reason I believe it was almost criminal that your death happened when it did. It was a few days before Christmas, the holiday you made so special in the hearts of your kids. Not only was it "the most wonderful time of the year" when we were forced to say goodbye, but the weather for your funeral was atrocious! Winter held its grip, and many of our family members from northern places couldn't make the trip. For the most honorable man I know, there were only a dozen people to celebrate your life.

Yet celebrate, we did. There was a twenty-one-gun salute, honoring your distinguished ten years of service as an Air Force police officer and a deputy sheriff. The first round elicited gasps from the family. The power of it overwhelmed some, but I felt only the honor and was thrilled to know you were being remembered this way. You received so many accommodations throughout your career. I believe you were especially fond of your time at SAC (Strategic Air Command) headquarters in Omaha, Nebraska, where you escorted dignitaries.

Then, my oldest niece gave birth to another one of your great grandchildren on Christmas Eve, a month earlier than expected, and just two days after your funeral. I pictured you looking down and celebrating with us. I like to think God took one of His children home but left our family with another child to soften the grief.

By the way, Christmas is still my favorite holiday. And that's thanks to the way you *lived*.

Lori

15

VIGILANCE

The highest form of love is to be the protector of another person's solitude. (Rainer Maria Rilke)

My Definition: Keeping persistent watch over someone or something, to protect against danger or struggle.

Origin: From the word *vigil*, or "watchful," and *vigilancy* in the 1530s, then the French word *vigilance* (sixteenth century) and Latin word *vigilantia* in the 1560s, which means, "wakefulness, watchfulness, attention."

Dad,

You were our protector. There is no better word to describe your dedication to the safety of our family. And as the quote above indicates, it's the highest form of love. After all, "Greater love has no one than this, that someone lay down his life for his friends" (John 15:13). I know in some regards, you did just that.

As I've gone through the catalogs of memories in my mind to write this book, Dad, so many of those memories had to do with vigilance and protection. I remember you carrying me around for at least a week after my calf sustained second-degree burns from an iron that fell from its board. Another memory took me to the time you pulled Mom and the four of us kids out of the car after it went into a ditch during a snowstorm. You got us to that farmhouse where we could call for help.

Speaking of snowstorms, do you remember the time after Grandma's funeral when you drove over seventy-five miles in white-out conditions for eleven hours to get us home safely? I chuckle now when I recall you coasting at about five miles per hour with your head out of the window to see the road because the wiper blades had frozen.

That's the thing. I can laugh about it now. We can all laugh because you kept us safe. Security was high on your list, and we felt that. We felt it through the little things and the big things.

And as a man of integrity, vigilance makes sense. John Calvin once said, "Integrity is the best of all protectors . . . we cannot be more secure than when fortified by a good conscience."

That's the truth. You kept us safe in the physical world; you also kept us safe in the emotional, social, and mental parts of this world too.

You were—*are*—my hero. A vigilant guard standing at the doorways of our lives. Ready. Waiting. *Loving.*

16

VULNERABILITY (PART I)

Only when we are brave enough to explore the darkness will we discover the infinite power of our light. (Brené Brown)

My Definition: Willingness to be exposed to attack or harm, either physically or emotionally.

Origin: From 1600 and the late Latin word *vulnerabilis,* meaning, "wounding," which was taken from early Latin *vulnerare,* "to wound, hurt, injure, maim."

Dad,
 After you passed away, Mom gave me a plastic

blue box—Carolina blue—filled with countless sticky notes that you had scribbled on during the last few months of your life. They were the messages you wrote once you lost your voice. Though I'd seen you with them from time to time, I didn't know what your notes said. Sometimes, I found a few lying around the house while you continued to battle ALS, but my energy was focused on you and your well-being, not those cryptic handwritten messages. So I never read them. I referred to them as your graffiti because I assumed no one would be able to understand the handwritten messages, at least not unless they knew you.

Over the last few years, I tried to open that box. The sticky notes seemed to call out to me, and I wondered what you'd jotted down in your final season on this earth. I usually didn't get too far, though. Every time I lifted the lid, I picked up the scent of your handkerchiefs, the faint whiff of fabric softener mixed with the smell of paper. Remember how you used to read two or three books at a time, Dad? Well, the smell of paper or old books reminds me of you. With each attempt, my quivering heart couldn't take it, so I abruptly replaced the top of the box.

As a result, those little pieces of paper became

grander and more significant in my thoughts and dreams. I imagined they contained wisdom and poignant life lessons—all the things I needed to carry on after you were gone. I fantasized, believing those sticky notes would provide me with many answers to life, and I envisioned crafting an entire book around those notes. I even titled it, *My Daddy's Graffiti*. I was sure I would know exactly what each message would mean because you and me, well, we got each other.

When I finally built up the courage to start my book project, I opened the box, retrieved the items, and read what I could. Painfully, I flipped through stacks of sticky notes, notebooks, greeting cards, the backside of the junk mail on which you wrote things, and the blood-stained napkins from your first trip to the hospital. Oh, Dad, those were the worst ones to revisit because I could tell you were afraid, disconnected, and somewhat paranoid.

As you know, I didn't find the life lessons, wisdom, or encouragement I envisioned would be there. Instead, I found the ramblings of someone facing certain death. It's clear to me now just how much the disease affected the way your mind worked and how this was the only way you could communicate your jumbled thoughts. It was a heartbreaking realization—that and the fact that you always kept a brave face for us until you couldn't keep it anymore.

Because of this discovery, I learned you might be one of the most virtuous people in the world. You protected us, even as we cared for you, while you expressed your fears the only way you knew how. You never complained. You simply waged the war against death inside your mind. And you stayed *Dad* through it all.

No, your wisdom wasn't left behind with ink and pencil on paper scraps. It was and continues to be etched onto my heart! Through those subtle lessons on fear, life, and death—inferred by what was *not said*, what you *didn't* write, and what you *couldn't* express—I learned you were vulnerable, as we all are. I'd rarely gotten to glimpse that side of you, but I realized with these notes, it was there all along.

I didn't find your memoirs, any stories of adventure, or the nuggets of wisdom I hoped to find in that box. What I found was someone facing the end of his life, someone who didn't want to leave his family . . . someone who would deeply miss us! I found a vulnerable human being. And it was the best lesson yet.

I finally recognized that you were not invincible. I was able to come to grips with the fact you had weaknesses and fears, just like we all do. Even the strongest and bravest battle the foe of fear and sometimes lose. After all, it took years for me to find the courage to open that box and learn this lesson from you.

And through your vulnerability, I reached a new depth of compassion. I get it now, Dad.

Lori

VULNERABILITY (PART II)

When we were children, we used to think that when we were grown-up we would no longer be vulnerable. But to grow up is to accept vulnerability. . . . To be alive is to be vulnerable.
(Madeleine L'Engle)

My Dear Dad,

Those last couple of years of your life were difficult and grew progressively worse with each passing month, all the way until your diagnosis that left us stunned and broken. It started off with small issues, like that raspy voice, which eventually led to your struggles with speaking, swallowing, and other challenges with your memory. Just typing this takes me back to one of the hardest seasons in my life, and my eyes are growing moist.

You sought many doctors during those last few

years as we tried to figure out what was wrong. Some were focused on your heart—but none knew your heart like we did—others on your kidneys, and still others on your lungs. It wasn't until mid-May, 2009, when one doctor finally listened to our concerns. He heard all the problems we listed and ran probing tests that went deeper to solve the mystery illness you were battling.

We found out that you had suffered a series of small strokes. TIAs they called them—transient ischemic attacks. I remember looking at the report with relief and thinking that we'd finally figured out what was going on. With the speech issues and your problems with swallowing, it all made sense, at least at that time. There's nothing more frustrating than knowing something is wrong, and then nothing more satisfying as having an answer that connects a series of different ailments. But, thankfully—though we were satisfied—your new doctor didn't want to stop there. He referred you to Duke Medical Center.

I had just graduated from Belmont Abbey College. My graduation was a day in the making for thirty years. How fantastic it was to have you and Mom there to see me receive my hard-earned diploma. By all appearances, Dad, you looked good; your weight, your color, and your demeanor were as they'd always been. *Healthy-looking.*

VULNERABILITY (PART II) | 73

On May 26, ten days later, I drove you and Mom to Duke for that appointment your doctor had scheduled for us. The drive was fun, filled with banter and joking among the three of us. While we knew this was the trip that would likely provide us with the final answers to so many of our questions from the last couple of years, no one would have been able to sense the weight of that day based on our cutting up and carrying on. And I'll take the memory of that car ride to Duke with me to my own grave.

After we arrived, you were taken back for a series of tests. Mom and I sat in the waiting room, chatting away as we always did. In my usual style of trying to make light of hard situations through my version of stark humor, I quoted Jim Morrison by saying, "No one here gets out alive." It was truly meant to be a small measure of realism turned into humor for our benefit. Oh, how I've looked back and regretted that moment many times over.

After several hours, around 3:00 p.m., Mom and I were called back to the doctor's office. You were sitting there, rigid, and as white as the T-shirt you wore. You didn't know anything yet, but I could tell that you were as frightened as you'd ever been.

Once we were all seated, the doctor began a methodical description of your medical history, what tests had been run that day, and his analysis of all things considered. I'm not sure any of us took a breath during that recitation. Today, all I recall is the agony I felt, the sensation of my stomach dropping, my face flushing, and my throat constricting, when the letters A . . . L . . . S . . . (ALS) came out of his mouth.

The doctor explained the usual symptoms and the reason it had been difficult for any one doctor to put the pieces together. This disease had not manifested in you as it usually does. There was also the issue of your age that complicated the diagnosis. You were a good thirty years older than most patients who receive the diagnosis. The doctor's words began to fade for all of us. I could tell you and Mom were busy digging through every memory or piece of knowledge you had about ALS. Most know the Lou Gerhig story, and I imagine that was front and center for both of you.

"Why didn't we know this sooner?" I asked the doctor when I could find words.

"Doctors are reluctant to give that diagnosis because of the impact it has on people's lives," the doctor replies. He then went on to explain the limitations the diagnosis carried: no more driving, for one. Dad, you barely said a word. Both you and Mom sat like deer in headlights.

Finally, I asked the question I dreaded the answer to. "How long does he have?"

With a deep breath, the doctor said, "It's hard to say. It could be months, or it could be years." The rest of the conversation trailed off. I have no memory of it.

But I'll never forget the look on the doctor's face as he laid out the results. He took his time so we could understand the full picture of the ALS diagnosis, even apologizing for what we would have to endure in the weeks and months to come. We stood (you sat) unmoving, barely breathing. The doctor asked if we needed to speak to anyone; we declined. He gave us all the time we needed as Mom reached for you.

"We just want to go home," I told the doctor as he turned to leave. After two years of symptoms and doctor visits without answers, ALS had never entered our minds. Shock's punch came out of nowhere.

After your doctor told us we would be in good hands at the Charlotte ALS clinic, we left with the weight of dread and uncertainty battling it out inside our hearts and souls. I asked for a wheelchair for you and went ahead to get the car. That shuffle down the longest hallway I'd ever seen and then out to the parking lot was the longest walk of my life. Longer,

Dad, than that walk to the back of the grocery store after I had scraped up the car as a new driver and hidden it from you thirty-two years before.

Shaken to my core, I couldn't yet cry so instead, I kept shuffling, eyes averted, unable to see anything. Only feel.

The chattiness and laughter we usually experienced on car rides were replaced with a steady stream of tears on the trip home. Tears, gasps, and pleading with God for answers: "Why this? Why us? What are we going to do?"

The road ahead was unknown—the amount of time together also unknown. Because of this, the fear was palpable! It weaved itself through the car, filling every space and sucking the oxygen we tried to inhale.

What was burned into my memory was your and Mom's crying that started the instant we closed the car doors. It came in waves, with starts and stops. Phone calls were made by Mom to each of my siblings. Each time the prognosis was proclaimed the painful crying started all over again. The sound rings in my ears even today, like a haunting melody. I was thankful you were both in the back seat so you couldn't see my sliding tears, wetting my cheeks on the way home too. I quickly wiped them away. The trauma and my emotional agony muffled so as not to add to your pain, but there just the same.

I stayed silent but not still, praying fervently inside my head and staring out the windshield as I drove. I wanted to be *strong*. As the oldest, I cherished my self-imposed duty to take care of you and Mom when the time came. I knew it was time. I wouldn't learn until much later how being brave and vulnerable is so much better than putting up a facade of strength.

Those may have been the only moments of authentic vulnerability you had, Dad. That ride home from Duke, where we spoke of so many *adult* things —life and death things—left a wildly important impression on me.

But after that, as your disease progressed, I didn't see the vulnerability. I didn't see you waging the war to live. As you lost your ability to speak, I grew angry. I'm sure most of it was directed at the disease and this fallen world, but I didn't understand why you weren't fighting back, either. That you seemed to give up. At times, my consternation overshadowed my connection with you.

Then, years later, your sticky notes in that long-closed box told me so much. They revealed every bit of your vulnerability—the precious virtue that tells each of us we are part of one humanity. I realized you had been communicating the only way you could. Frustration, even new anger directed toward myself, leaped to the surface as I pulled each note out and tried to decipher your fear-based messages.

On the notes, your handwriting became difficult to read, nearly illegible over time. I could see a change in your thought process too—even the thoughts themselves morphed as the ALS took hold. Your notes became shorter, fragmented, and more cryptic. What they told me was that you were afraid. And I hate that I didn't see that sooner. I was so focused on what you didn't have anymore—and what I didn't have anymore—instead of what you were *still giving us*. Oh, Dad, I am so sorry for feeling that frustration and anger and for losing so many precious days that we can't get back now. I wish I could go back in time. I wish I could give you a hug.

My own vulnerability has been a work in progress ever since. Your wisdom whispers still.

Lori

18

INTEGRITY

Integrity is a life where your beliefs and intentions are aligned with your words and actions. (Stephen Longrove)

My Definition: Firm adherence to a code of moral values.

Origin: From the 1400s, *integrite* meant "innocence, blamelessness; chastity, purity," from the Old French word, *integrité,* and directly from the Latin word, *integritatem* (nominative *integritas*), meaning "soundness, wholeness, completeness;" and figuratively, meaning "purity, correctness, blamelessness," from *integer*, "whole."

Dear Dad,

The months that followed your diagnosis were filled with periods of adjustment and busyness: setting appointments with the ALS clinic, working with the Disabled Veterans Association to get you established to receive benefits, and buying equipment to help with your speech and eating. The many tasks and appointments kept Mom so busy that she didn't dwell on the inevitable. You, on the other hand, were consumed with the future. You could see it a little more every day, and you seemed to have given up and given in.

In early July, we went to the ALS clinic. You were struggling to breathe that day. As a reformed smoker, this happened from time to time, but it had never escalated to the degree it was that day. The doctor said your oxygen was low, that you needed to go to the emergency room right away.

I have no idea what was in my head when I suggested we walk the two blocks from the clinic to the hospital. Looking back, I can only guess shock had taken over my brain and left me unable to make any wise decisions. That walk was so difficult for you, but once we started, you said we should just keep going. When we arrived, they immediately admitted you and put you on oxygen.

I believe you had pneumonia, but what was more

apparent was your cognitive condition. Your thoughts and words were scattered, disoriented, and agitated. I asked the doctor if Alzheimer's disease could suddenly appear, and if so, was this it? That was my only point of reference for the way you were acting.

The team did some cognitive testing and confirmed it wasn't Alzheimer's but likely the effects of the ALS on your frontal lobe. Those were an awful four days for you, Dad. I hate you had to go through them.

After your release, things rapidly sped downhill. Breathing machines, feeding machines, ALS clinic visits, and more chaos filled our days.

We decided to have your and Mom's fiftieth wedding anniversary party a month before your actual anniversary because we didn't know what condition you would be in. Over thirty people attended that party. You had as great a time as you could, being the usual "card" you always were.

October arrived, and you were again admitted to the hospital.

Dad, as difficult a prayer as it was, my plea was for God to take you Home to be with Him. I didn't want to deal with Halloween. The memories around that holiday should stay fun and lighthearted. The continued phone calls from loved ones brought us all anxiety. What was there to say? And Mom didn't know what to do . . .

In early November, Mom had the realization that your time was truly limited. It was devastating to watch. Hospice was notified, yet you hung on.

On December 18, I had lunch with some of my Christian friends, and I shared my feeling that you wouldn't be with us on Christmas. It was just an intuition, perhaps a nudge from the Holy Spirit to help me prepare my heart.

December 19, 2009 came.

That morning, I went to your house as I had done every other day for the past several months. You lay in the hospital bed in your bedroom, as you had done for most of the days that made up the past month or two. I told Mom to get out of the house for a bit—that I'd sit with you.

Once she left, the house grew quiet. As I sat at the side of your bed, I wasn't sure if you could hear me. Still, I chatted about my morning, the weather, everyone's anticipation of Christmas—all the small talk you do when someone can't talk back. I remembered I had a pamphlet in my purse (I don't know where I got it), but it was about the story of Joseph and Mary's journey to Bethlehem and the birth of Jesus. Since it was so quiet sitting there, silent enough to compare to the silent night that became the most Holy night over 2000 years before, I pulled out the pamphlet.

Your breathing became shallow, labored. I wondered if it was your position in bed, the effects of the morphine, or something else. I rubbed the top of your bruised hand, then squeezed it. The slightest movement in your warm yet frail fingers told me you knew I was there. Never in my life had I read a Bible story to you, Dad—or to anyone in my family, except to my kids. But that day, I did. I lifted the pamphlet and shared the story of our Lord's birth. I spoke slowly and deliberately so you could hear each step of Joseph and Mary's journey. I prayed you felt the hope of restoration found in Jesus's birth.

The Birth of Jesus Christ

In those days a decree went out from Caesar Augustus that all the world should be registered. This was the first registration when Quirinius was governor of Syria. And all went to be registered, each to his own town. And Joseph also went up from Galilee, from the town of Nazareth, to Judea, to the city of David, which is called Bethlehem, because he was of the house and lineage of David, to be registered with Mary, his betrothed, who was with child. And while they were there, the time came for her to give birth. And she gave birth to her firstborn son and wrapped him in swaddling cloths and laid him in a manger, because there was no place for them in the inn.

The Shepherds and the Angels

And in the same region there were shepherds out in the field, keeping watch over their flock by night. And an angel of the Lord appeared to them, and the glory of the Lord shone around them, and they were filled with great fear. And the angel said to them, "Fear not, for behold, I bring you good news of great joy that will be for all the people. For unto you is born this day in the city of David a Savior, who is Christ the Lord. And this will be a sign for you: you will find a baby wrapped in swaddling cloths and lying in a manger." And suddenly there was with the angel a multitude of the heavenly host praising God and saying,

   "Glory to God in the highest,
   and on earth peace among those with whom he is pleased!"

When the angels went away from them into heaven, the shepherds said to one another, "Let us go over to Bethlehem and see this thing that has happened, which the Lord has made known to us." And they went with haste and found Mary and Joseph, and the baby lying in a manger. And when they saw it, they made known the saying that had been told them concerning this child. And all who heard it wondered at what the shepherds told them. But Mary treasured up all these things, pondering them in her heart. And the shepherds returned, glorifying and praising God for all they had heard and seen, as it had been told them (Luke 2:1–20).

Until a few months before your passing, I did not know how you felt about Jesus, heaven, or forgiveness. You were always a good person—a virtuous person—and always gave so much for your family, never broke a law, etc., but I never knew how you felt about God. A couple of months before you died, you shared with me an idea. "No longitude, no latitude, that's heaven."

That's all I had from you because of your struggles with your speech, but I knew in that moment, you had discovered Jesus. I saw the change in you. Then, as I read you that story beside your hospital bed, the all-consuming quiet was replaced with peace. The stillness was no longer overwhelming but suddenly holy.

The day progressed as it normally did. Your meds were given at the appointed times, and whispered conversations took place outside your room; we received calls from extended family to see how you were doing. Hospice had arrived the day before. You were newly shaven and your hair neatly lay in place, silver and clean. Dad, you were always particular about your hair! I knew you would be happy to know that you looked handsome, even when you were so sick.

In all my adult life, I'd never stayed the night with Mom and you. That day, I felt I needed to. There was nothing different about that day that would have prompted my decision to stay—just a feeling that I should be there.

About 8:20 that evening, Mom and I were eating ice cream and watching something on TV that made us laugh. I heard a sound, maybe a shutter, from your room. I could see your bed from my spot in the living room. All looked as it had all day.

Several minutes later, Mom took the dishes into the kitchen, and I went to check on you. As I entered the room, I could feel the air had changed. The quiet had been replaced with heaviness. Your shallow breathing was gone. Dad, *you* were gone. I stared at your earthly body for what felt like hours. In one thought, I couldn't believe you were gone, then in the next, I thanked God that He'd taken you Home. No more pain, just peace.

As Mom came down the hall, I told her you had passed. She stared in disbelief, then broke down. I knew she was reliving fifty years in a single moment.

Her world changed in that instant, the second she knew she'd lost you.

The calls began, the ambulance came, then the quiet returned. Once I got Mom into bed, I lay there on the coach, staring into your empty bedroom. I was overcome with more weighty silence and the most numbing fog I've ever experienced. I was spent!

I lay there sad but so very grateful for you, Dad.

19

A LETTER FROM DAD

Six months before his death, the only recorded entry in his journal, dated June 9

"I asked myself all the time why I was spared from death several times in my life: when stung more than thirty times by hornets at ten years old when climbing a tree; when having double pneumonia and given [my] last rights at seventeen (this was the time I'm certain I'd had an out-of-body experience); when I couldn't get my duffle bag off the plane and had to wait for the next plane (two other airmen who could get off the plane caught a C-119, which a short time later crashed and killed everyone on board); and while stationed in [Morocco], we were at a bomb dump blowing bad ammunition when a piece of shrapnel missed me by inches.

I finally found out in May that I would not be spared this time. I was told I had an incurable disease. At first, I was angry—WHY ME?! Then I prayed to the Lord, and He said, 'Why not?"

I'm just a simple man that loves and adores my wife Marti, [my] kids, and [my] grandchildren.

I finally know that without her love, my family, and God, I would never have known this beautiful life and understand what it's all about.

I am not afraid to die, but I sure will miss you all. I will say my prayers tonight.

If I shouldn't wake tomorrow, you'll know why I didn't write more in this journal. Your mom and Lori are conservators—Mom for knowing us and Lori for knowing God."

20

THE LAST WORD

A virtue is a beneficial character trait that helps us succeed and protects us from harm. Our virtues lay the foundation for us to live morally good lives. Everyone has virtues, but not all our virtues are the same. We're born with certain virtuous character traits, and others we learn along the way.

I was gifted with several virtues through my dad, both genetically and because of the way he treated my mom, parented us, and, in general, took care of his family and respected those around him. The ones I outlined in these letters to heaven are the ones most easily recognized in my dad throughout this life. He also displayed humility (quietly sharing his accolades over dinner), loyalty (he and my mom were married over fifty years!), and responsibility (working third shifts and sometimes more than one job so he could be there for his five children, which he had before the age of twenty-seven). These virtues just oozed out of his daily coming and going.

Dad was obedient to his God too. However, religion and faith were private affairs—we didn't discuss these things until this last season in his life, after his ALS diagnosis, when the time for him to transition to his heavenly home was fast approaching.

It's been an honor to share these stories with you, highlighting my dad's goodness and legacy. And that's one of the most important truths—that these are his *legacy*. They will be passed down from generation to generation, just as he likely learned them from his parents and grandparents.

My mom expressed our ongoing grief the best in one of her journal entries from August 2010, many months after his passing:

I have to write this down. Fifty years I was married to Jack. Not once did he deny me anything. Now I have to come to the reality that he's not coming back to me. I'm so mad that he's denying me this. He was my special gift in life. To this day, I don't know what I did to deserve him. It's so hard letting him go, and it's very possible I never will. Nobody told me when I married him that I would have to give him up one day. I hope he's being taken good care of now.

My dad was a gift to all who knew him.

I hope and pray you, dear reader, don't live one more minute without telling the people you love how special they are. I hope you don't go another day without saying "I love you" or "thank you." Most of all, I hope you don't wait until the end to live a life full of love, peace, and joy. Don't leave anything unsaid; carry no regrets.

I implore you . . . live like this man of integrity and tell the people in your life how much they mean to you.

MORE ON ALS AND THE INTIMATE IMPACT

Amyotrophic Lateral Sclerosis (ALS) is a neurological and neuromuscular disease that affects people of all races and ethnic backgrounds, though Caucasian and non-Hispanic males have a higher incidence. It affects the nerve cells that control our voluntary muscle movements (those muscles we choose to move). The symptoms get worse over time. Muscle twitches turn into muscle cramps; weakness becomes paralysis, and slurred speech and difficulty swallowing progress to an inability to talk (as in the case of my dad) or eat. Individuals with ALS eventually lose the ability to breathe on their own and turn to ventilators to keep them alive.

According to the ALS Association, approximately 5,000 people in the US are diagnosed with ALS each year, which averages to about fifteen new cases each day. Although the average life expectancy of a person with ALS is about two to five years from the time of diagnosis, some people can live with the disease for more than five years. Typically, those are the people who have the financial resources to continue the costly treatments and advanced technologies.

Speaking of treatments and technologies, this generic overview speaks to the somewhat rare incidence of ALS but not to the intimate impact of ALS on the individuals and their loved ones. While a small percentage are afflicted (as compared to cancer or Alzheimer's disease), their journeys and the journeys of their support network are heartbreaking. The disease is personal, traumatic, and life-changing.

When I shared with others that my dad had been diagnosed with ALS, the resounding response was a *gasp* followed by a breathy, "I'm . . . so . . . sorry." At the time, I didn't know why I was getting that response, but I came to deeply understand the gravity of those gasps.

Our story is just one story about someone who battled ALS. But it's *our* story. This journey changed us; it changed me.

At the cornerstone, my dad lost his ability to speak, and to a degree, to communicate with clarity and meaning. Speech deficits and dementia are just a few affects people with ALS might suffer. Dad was well-read and knowledgeable. He loved to share his thoughts and ideas and was good at debating, that is until his convictions were challenged.

I've spent many an hour contemplating what it must feel like to lose your voice. No, I'm not talking about our First Amendment rights but the ability to audibly convey our thoughts, feelings, concerns, desires, and dreams. I'm referring to losing the ability to communicate the essence of who we are as people. As loved ones. I cannot imagine.

Over the last several months of Dad's life, he scribbled on Post-it notes and notepads. Some of those notes could be deciphered, and some were short glimpses into the inner world of a desperate, sometimes confused, man facing his mortality.

Dad knew he would pass from this disease, but he never spoke about it. He didn't spend those last few months imparting wisdom and lessons to his children. Impending death is a funny thing. Some will embrace it as Morrie did (I'm referencing *Tuesdays with Morrie*) or Randy Pausch in *The Last Lecture*, or Steve Jobs in his final season of life. I desperately wanted my dad to share his stories like they did, but I never pressed him on that.

Then a realization hit: His transference of life lessons happened more subtly, in casual conversations throughout the years leading up to his diagnosis, in trips down memory lane we took as a family when he was well, and, of course, toward the end, he lived out the hardest virtue to teach, vulnerability, through the hundreds of little sticky notes he left behind.

It's the love for my father and for all of my family that I've shared these stories in the spirit that I believe he'd want to share them.

If you or a loved one has been diagnosed with ALS, my heart and prayers go out to you.

For more information about ALS, check out these resources:

- ALS Association: the largest, national, non-profit organization dedicated to ALS support and research.
- MDA ALS: supports muscular dystrophy and related life-threatening diseases, such as ALS, through its national network of clinics.
- National Institutes of Health (NIH)
- I AM ALS: patient-led community that provides critical support and resources to patients, caregivers, and loved ones.

ACKNOWLEDGMENTS

Thank you to my Lord and Savior, who instilled in my heart the yearning to soothe the hearts of others by sharing my stories. Through His grace, I have discovered vulnerability, healing, and peace.

To my husband Clint, my best friend and biggest fan, whose support is unwavering. Thank you for always being there for me!

Thank you to my children and grandchildren, who inspired me to share these memories of the wonderful man they called "Bumpa" and to indulge me by listening to all my storytelling throughout their lives. I'm truly blessed to be your mom and nana.

To my "sisterhood," who unconditionally encourages my endless dreams and aspirations.

Many thanks to my editor, Cortney Donelson, for helping me re-shape a decade-long dream to honor my dad. It's amazing what can grow out of an hour-long chat outside of a café on a sunny day!

OTHER BOOKS BY LORI MYERS

Glimpses of Tenderness: Soothing the Soul Through Reminiscence

Change, Creativity, Curiosity, and Hope in a Crisis Called Pandemic; poetry and short stories by members of Writing Bootcamp Charlotte

Why Do We Love? When Love Works, When it Doesn't, When it Settles; poetry and short stories by American Writers

Belmont Abbey College *Agora*

Montreat College literary magazine

ABOUT THE AUTHOR

Lori Myers is a wife, mother, grandmother, sister, daughter, and friend! Her greatest loves are faith and family! She has a passion for writing that provokes emotion and for coaching people to discover their full potential by exploring possibilities. She holds a Master's Degree from Montreat College in Management and Leadership, a Bachelor's Degree in Liberal Studies from Belmont Abbey College, and enjoys a career in information technology. Lori lives outside Charlotte, North Carolina, with her husband, Clint.

www.ingramcontent.com/pod-product-compliance
Lightning Source LLC
Chambersburg PA
CBHW021115080526
44587CB00010B/530